Nesting Doll

Nesting Doll

Rita Brady Kiefer

University Press of Colorado

Copyright © 1999 by the University Press of Colorado
International Standard Book Number 0-87081-548-2

Published by the University Press of Colorado
P.O. Box 849
Niwot, Colorado 80544

The University Press of Colorado is a cooperative publishing enterprise sup-
ported, in part, by Adams State College, Colorado State University, Fort Lewis
College, Mesa State College, Metropolitan State College of Denver, University of
Colorado, University of Northern Colorado, University of Southern Colorado,
and Western State College of Colorado.

The paper used in this publication meets the minimum requirements of the
American National Standard for Information Sciences — Permanence of Paper
for Printed Library Materials. ANSI Z39.48-1984

Library of Congress Cataloging-in-Publication Data

Kiefer, Rita, 1930–
    Nesting doll / Rita Brady Kiefer.
      p.   cm.
    ISBN 0-87081-548-2 (alk. paper)
    1. Women Poetry. 2. Ex-nuns Poetry. I. Title.
PS3561.I338N47   1999
811'.54—dc21   99-41313
                                                        CIP

Book design by Laura Furney

08 07 06 05 04 03 02 01 00 99   10 9 8 7 6 5 4 3 2 1

. . . to the women of A Woman's Place

. . . to all the dolls nesting

. . . again and above all — Jerry

Contents

Acknowledgments

I wish to thank and acknowledge the editors of the following journals and magazines in which certain poems in this manuscript first appeared: *Buffalo Bones:* "Writers Debate"; *Calopooya Collage:* "Exorcism"; *The Guadalupe Review:* "Broken Woman On The Wall"; *The International Poetry Review:* "About Mortification" from "Sister Mailee Sequence"; *The Kansas Quarterly:* "Rice Pudding"; *Many Mountains Moving:* "Like This" and "Ex-Nun in a Red Mercedes"; *The Spoon River Poetry Review:* "Prophecy"; *Weber Studies:* "Certain Words"; *The Windless Orchard:* "Exorcism"; *The Writer's Voice:* "Ex-Nun In A Red Mercedes."

"Ex-Nun In A Red Mercedes," "Last Song," "One More Woman Who Wouldn't Talk Back" (under the title "Disbelief"), "Sister Mailee Sequence" appeared in *Unveiling* (Chicory Blue Press, 1993); "Rice Pudding" appeared in *Trying On Faces* (Monkshood Press, 1995). Special acknowledgment and gratitude to the publishers of the respective presses: Sondra Zeidenstein and Deena Larsen.

Grateful acknowledgment also to the editors of *The National Poetry Competition Winners' Anthology* (The Chester H. Jones Foundation, 1991) in which "Rapture" appeared.

This collection of poems is made possible in part by support from the College of Arts and Sciences, University of Northern Colorado and by grants from the Graduate School at that institution. Additional assistance was provided by a grant from the Colorado Council on the Arts and by an Associateship with the Rocky Mountain Women's Institute.

I thank those whose generosity and careful readings over the years helped me: Dr. Becky Edgerton, Rick Proctor, Stephanie Moran, Joyce Flores-Kiefer, Karen Kiefer, Mary Crow, and my students from the creative writing classes at the University of Northern Colorado. Most of all the deepest gratitude to Jerry — my partner/husband and closest friend — for being who he is and for his assistance and enduring support.

Nesting Doll

One

EX-NUN IN A RED MERCEDES

Great car I tell my friend as we speed from
the convent, my shaved head
barely sprouting stubble, stuttering hands
not a clue what to do with the seatbelt, one of
many inventions conjured to save the body
those 18 years my own was on ice.
The nuns concocted less sophisticated, more
moral means, hence more everlasting: the veil,
13 layers of clothes, claw-pronged chains for the knee
and 33 strokes with knotted cords reminiscent of
other brandings — I am reminded as the dark red
grosgrain belts hum their automatic blessing over heart
belly and that place *down there* Ann O'Leary's mother called
our shame — my mother gave it no name, my mother never spoke
of it at all — yes, I recall the convent's calculations.
Something about this soft red fur against my spine
reminds me of redemption: no more examens,
accusations, chapters of fault and
      no more genuflections.
My knees convinced me to leave
somehow before the mind they knew the collusion:
mind tricking body, the body
      how far will this sabotage go.
Something about this red Mercedes and the mind
that didn't say *leave* until the female blood stopped
flowing — I was that in love with a phantom, that afraid
my body would betray me, that afraid of a man's near flesh, afraid
through some open summer window I might follow young favorites:
I'll Be Seeing You or better, worse, *As Time Goes By*
invading the body more than *Panis Angelicus*.
In this red, red car today speeding down Cleveland's Euclid
I am improvising songs for my beautiful body,
hymns to the geometry of bone and flesh and blood
I will find   again   and again   and again.

EXORCISM

This is to tell the hostess at
the Ramada Inn with a facelift that
in a room of empty tables I did not want
a corner one with dim lights where
she moved me from the booth for four
with space and red cushions,
soft and sensual under my bare thighs, under
the white gabardine shorts I wear on
vacations when trying to write
                          that I indeed ordered a Coors
not vanilla ice cream, that
I wanted really to sit in the restaurant
not as she suggested to retreat to
the bar where you can't see blank
pages, on this hot July afternoon or
orange fingernails that could
mark a woman's life.

RAPTURE

Still the woman from Avila,
how light her body drifting from its chapel
stall, the other nuns flinging themselves like
affectionate harpies to hold it down.
Teresa with her actual grace
hair after hair bristling, almost sizzling
from the heat her body carried. *Divine*
she called that light.

That light.   We all want it.
Is anything worth saying without it?

Yet suppose it was longing for
the almond she loved or the pepper
that took her off the ground
or river spasms in April
not any Lord at all, but
the world and words like God
kept rushing.

LAST SONG

I piece the divine fragments into the mandala
Whose center is the lost creative power.
                    —*Kathleen Raine*

Just before they cut out her tongue
she cried I will learn to *sign*, her
fingers lacing the air   he commanded
those hands silent   they brought cleavers
and ten spokes — a mandala — wailed red
on the cutting board. At 4 a.m.
the third day she began whistling
a score so original, one of them
ordered — his eyes on her lips — *bring*
me a peeler.

When they reached her heart
it was humming.

6

ONE MORE WOMAN WHO WOULDN'T TALK BACK

He dubbed my last song excessive
overdone, a bit hard to believe
the part about her tongue cut out, her lips
shredded by a peeler.
                              But I saw
the night they brought her home
the madman couldn't get enough
of her dear mouth, lust never tainting
that pure rage that made him
bite down so hard he didn't know
whose hot rush filled his mouth.
          When the prosecutor brought
a piece in a jar — no blood
just a swollen pink bladder —
only then did he seem to know
what he'd done.

MONOLOGUE

I talk to you everywhere: under sheets in the shower in the most
private places on the freeway (a passing car gestures) between the
foreword & p.1 culling rice grains from last night's spill everywhere:
on java joint patios in the kitchen rolling dough for a *Small Planet* pie
          (wax paper & flour with mama at nine)   inside a failed e-
mail an unanswered note   EVERY WHERE door after door closes
in the *No* play your face in the wings   from my pores your sweat
your grief at the river   (outside the library that small tree
4maybe5timescutdown keeps remembering)   sometimes
desperate for a voice I plead a sign but you just numb like
Rilke's mute doll   still   everywhere
I talk to you   talk to you   my sweet
diaphanous   my irrevocable
dead.

Epilogue: The dead they got all the eyes
          —William Kennedy.

KUDZU

(kudzu was brought from Japan in the thirties)

Frame 1:
what terrible beauty weaving like a drunk
curtain, its smooth pods wrapping
trees, fence posts, everything in its way

Frame 2:
it could have arrived while I was being born
curling its dark way from Japan
like incense or the snuffed twin candles at Kaddush

Frame 3
in the labor room the doctor tells
mother, *be careful what you say*
words make things happen

Frame 4:
it could have nested its perennial
seed in my mother's ear
her mother's or mine

Frame 5:
can you play your mother? the therapist asks
I say *yes* and begin washing miscarriage stains
four times from the same yellow dress then

Frame 6:
her voice haunting: *my sweet stillborn*
good-bye, you too my three-day-old darling,
go down deep in the plot, cruel boy

Frame 7:
see how it alters by its black-green explosion
its insatiable spreading, until nothing can hold
back its roots tenacious as the dead-mother-plot

BROKEN WOMAN ON THE WALL

for Angélica Gorodischer

At night I saw myself in pieces on the opposite wall,
a cardboard puzzle: left breast, ring finger, one eye
glazed like the damned on the Sistine ceiling.

Doctor-god, inscrutable conductor, you closed my voice-box
down. On paper I cursed you, shattered
the delicate steel baton you used to silence me,
turned it on you then scattered your bones
all through Argentina. I posted your photo
on municipal boards
labeled *wanted.*

Still one day I found wings and a new place
to sing from somewhere under the rib cage
behind the mask's bright humming.
For months the song grew: a grunt, a whisper.
Friends applauded. The technician, the therapist
waved and clapped, laughed with me, wept until
one day from the wall my voice broke out
praising all the broken parts.

RICE PUDDING

Last week in the mail I found your gift
recipe for rice pudding, today at the door
some Kokoho Rose rice for me
for my lover a book about rocks.
Did you know I'd abandon the kitchen for *Webster*?
rice led nowhere, nor *rocks*, so
I turned to *pudding*
and found *pudding stone: a conglomerate*.

Now pudding bakes in stoneware
waiting for what is trying to happen
in the space between swelling grains, in
the down-deep porous clay.

DEBATE

It takes an ego of
whalebone he says
or none she replies.

The old debate: *doors propel,*
windows are passive he scorns
she says *windows reveal*

my body can permeate glass
coax anything, anything inside
and she has the last word.

EXPERTS

River trips ruined through the binoculars
of the resident Audubon authority
her litany fating the birds

or hikes through canyons diminished
as the Guide expounds
confirming the stones

(in tenth grade biology
I wanted to be the amoeba
not diagram it)

and those literary priests
from their altar of truth
ordaining fiction as theory

we keep getting it wrong
experts don't name things
they stammer their love.

LIKE THIS

Don't try to explain the miracle, kiss me
on the lips, like this, like this.
                                        —*Rumi*

Not the way father kissed mother
on the cheek, not in the front of the house,
no, in the back, in the bedroom, basement, in
those dark places, those under the earth
places no one can see, kiss me
across mountains when we are apart, kiss me
under sly sheets after the trace of a late shower
kiss me the sweet, sweet kiss of the glad-we-are-married
on the lips. Once more. Once more. Kiss me
on the ear, not like the grackle or Canada jay
saying what's on its mind, like the hummingbird
laughing at gravity. Kiss me slow, not the way
aging bones explain marrow to each other
winter mornings. No. Slow. Like a late June
two-step. Oh I know   I know: time is
the only kiss that lasts, but
just now — tonight — make me
believe the miracle of lips
like this, like this

Two

SISTER MAILEE SEQUENCE

Prelude: *in the voice of St. Therese of Lisieux, the Little Flower*

I know all about fading. Remember
those petals I tossed from heaven. They're dim
on the edges now.   A father who gave me to God
before I could write my own name, before my breasts
could make the most of blousing.
Think of it — little Therese Martin fixed at age three.
Cats and me!   *Dedicated*, they said,
she'll be our little nun, our saint some day.
Therese of Lisieux, chosen by God,
every family needs a chosen.
What a cheap heaven-ticket! but
he always could sniff a bargain,
especially a holy one, my father.

The nuns refused you medicine?

It was God's will.

They weren't stopped?

You don't just stop God.   Besides
I was destined to suffer, make reparation.

Reparation?   For what?

Who knows?
They said my sickness was a sign.
The younger we die, the greater the praise!

I believed in small things.
They dubbed me "Saint of the Unspectacular."
At 15 a Carmelite, at 24 a Saint.
A dead saint. Canonized.
Every family wants one.

What do you want, Therese?

What do I want? I want a new face
a new fate this time. This time
not a saint.

1. Female Jesuits

I know that if at this moment I had before me a group of twenty young
Germans singing Nazi songs in chorus, a part of my soul would instantly
become Nazi. This is a very great weakness, but that is how I am. . . .
                                                                Simone Weil

In my blue corner room, I am saying good-bye
to the dark walnut secretary desk, faithful
hiding place for secrets since I turned twelve
six years of diaries and journals
thick with accusations or friendships on trial
reconcilings fragile as the pansies and phlox
and lilies-of-the-valley bordering these pages.

Part of a life will flame soon from the metal
basket on the side stone porch of the magnolia
house. No one will find my words. One burning
then   pffff!   all will be ashes, all
the pages blank.

If we hadn't moved, if I had gone
to the other girls' school at the end of
Belmore Road in East Cleveland but
daddy wanted the Magnolia house.
          Destiny pointed me six blocks down Liberty
Boulevard to Notre Dame Academy for Girls, 248
gabardine uniforms, 248 ninth-grade heads
stiff as our detachable collars starched
white on navy blue. At first assembly Sister Ralph
said we would be taught by *female Jesuits*
Ignatius Loyola style. Years later I would remember
that first day feeling like Stephen Daedalus looking for

his name on a geography flyleaf, and dreaming
James Joyce's somewhere-green-rose that blossoms.

Good-bye, blue vanity, your kidney-shaped top
glass like the cracked one on daddy's desk when I was five.
No! No! No! I shook at the interrogation
and wondered if he could see inside my head
the way God did my heart, straight down to the lie.
Everyone's a watcher, even in sleep.

Flex your muscles Daddy coaxed, then
nicknamed me *Pete* so I signed notes
with the dead infant's name buried deep
in the family plot, the dead infant
who might have been priest-son
to my Irish daddy.   Instead he got a girl
and today that daughter is leaving
the world, the devil, the flesh
to be — next best to priest — a nun.

> Dick O. should see her body now,
> those legs he said had *most potential
> climbing stairs*, veiled in black lisle
> primed for cloister life.
> She remembered that night the first mirror talked:
> *give it to God, your body spells trouble.*   Or
> the morning — she was five — Mr. Barth tossed her
> high in the churchyard air, that pink dress
> naughty as a windy umbrella.
> *She'll get in trouble with those eyes,* he said
> just before he caught her, and
> all through Mass she hid her face.
> *Always blaming me for what they do!*

> > *(Silly you men — so very adept
> > at wrongly faulting womankind
> > not seeing you're alone to blame
> > for faults you plant in woman's mind.)*
> > (Sor Juana)

19

2. Elevator Ride to the Cloister

At five I would ask mother, how come
I call me *I* ? Everybody else says *she.*

Never at home on the ground.   At eighteen flying
to the cloister. Good-bye world! The same tug
from the bottom, the same start as the ferris wheel
rides in Asbury Park summers.   But this gate is safer
its accordion metal *click* and the elevator's straight climb.
No return-wheel this time.   Floor by floor like
Thomas Merton's seven-story mountain or
the Saint of Avila's seven mansions.
Destination: Cloister.   A sign I'd seen daily
as an Academy girl, its black and white
four-cornered seduction: *Cloister.   Private.*
Like private parts, I thought, the first time.
                Like borderlines, ultimatums.
I almost changed the rules on the dim side porch
with Dick O. that night.   Almost.   Maybe it was
the miraculous medal pinned to my slip
for protection, or the scapular's prickle
just before he tried to cross over to
that place Joan O'Leary's mother called
our shame.   My own mother called it no name.
My own mother never spoke of it at all.

It will be different when we move she said.
But mother never wanted the big house.
It was daddy restless after promotion
the girls too big for the yellow and red
wallpaper children skipping rope, too old
for a chamber pot in their bedroom, the regular
toilet forbidden because *daddy is a light sleeper.*
Daddy who still sleeps light in the family plot
he planned.   Even the large chestnut
growing beside him conformed.   But in the end
a boulder wouldn't let his body down.

20

Mother grew quiet in the big magnolia house.
I'm losing my hair, she would say. Thirteen years
after Mr. Barth and daddy, my diary complained:
I'm not gonna live like mother.
I've decided to marry God.

Hour bells from the tower drown
the foreign sounds on entrance day
summoning a white-veiled novice fated as
my "guardian angel" who makes the elevator
to the fourth-floor stop humming, its frosted
glass door opens like a winter womb
and I slide all the way into the cloister
just after smoothing my bangs in the brass
panel sprouting numbers. But I am not
that postulant, that body shrouded in black.
Someone else gleams back.
I am dimming.

3. Wings and Fur

At five they found my pet canary frozen in
father's study, the coldest room in the house.
I got up from scarlet fever and
they had buried him. Death by freezing.
Even then I knew: we never stop grieving.

When my yellow bird died I turned
my face to the wall.   At five I was that bird and

> *lily-of-the-valley, scarlet poppy,*
> *bubble, stone for the pocket, at five pushing through*
> *feather   pistil   stamen   translucent wall*
> *plucking — those days — feathers and petals one by one.*

Grandma invented the wings sprouting in my mirror.
If they belonged to an angel why were they that shade?
Grandma never saw them black, Grandma never

heard the beast, the one with all the voices,
its eyes dark as my black triangle, my black fur.
Why — even though my hair was the color of honey — why
did my triangle stay so black?

Such a cross-breeding: beast and angel.
Such a holy communion.

4. About Mortification

On the fourth day they issued numbers.
Hers was *101.*
She'd heard about absolute zero and
one.

Except for roses or mums or asters
at Benediction or the chaplain's hands sprouting
deep blond hairs against his right-season vestment,
no color fretted the cloister, but in the middle of
those Nocturnal Adoration nights
before the exposed Host she'd come quick
from sleep to the chapel dizzy with roses and
ivory beeswax, to a front pew near the gold
monstrance exploding, its round glass pyx holding the holy wafer.
Nights of blue-white stars flung over Madison-on-the-Lake
that last summer her bathing suit white as eternity
with all its possibilities.
At communion next morning the priest's hands
man-hands raising the host. She would practice
custody of the eyes. Since age five, eyes and sex
like growths in a Petri dish. Now she could
banish them both with the Rule.
The Rule that shaped each act: how to
fold a towel, place pins in a veil, stack
all-facing-left prayer books in chapel pews.
And rules for the body: *the Sisters shall conceal hands
in sleeves to avoid swinging their worldly arms.*
The Rule at first a foreign language now her mentor.

Holy Rule, help me expel the devil,
that damned ventriloquist.

> She tried open prongs of
> the penance chain, to mortify her flesh
> right above the knee and Friday flagellations
> with the discipline's knotted cord: 33 strokes
> each arm each year of the Jesus life.
> On feastdays she'd take two fewer olives,
> a mere half piece of cake.

> Yet under her postulant cape the irony of
> silk blouses flattering her full breasts.
> Who'd see them now? She needed to know
> if Dick O. drove by in his old Chevy
> would she still feel crepe de Chine clinging?

> Her shredded poems fed the incinerator when
> Sister Superior cautioned: *don't become proud.*
> When did the questions stop?
> The day she denied Father Daugherty's stares?
> the night she burned her words? or
> when the female blood stopped flowing?
> Or was it that Indian summer night in her cell
> she prayed to die October third at age twenty,
> four years younger than the Little Flower of Lisieux.

5.   Sister Mailee Goes All The Way With Jesus

> The Chinese name for Mary: Mailee so liquid and
> lyrical.   Mailee. Tomorrow her new name and
> investment with the Bride of Christ veil.
> But tonight was shearing time.

> This shedding was private as any first loss
> white muslin drawn — against intruders — on
> all four sides of her cell. Steel blades poised
> in Sister Elreda's right hand, in her left,
> electric clippers.

Just below the ears or
do you want to go all the way with Jesus?

Her eyes closed to block the electric hum,
she called back other women
who had let themselves be shorn: Catherine of Sienna,
Teresa of Avila, Francis of Assisi's Claire,
and those in camps, shaved out of shame
while she was learning to divide and multiply
and have her first periods. And mother,
stunned when they shaved her
pubic hair before the dead baby, mother
whose raven hair had grown brilliant
brushing her blond child's singular curls.
Later Mother's quiet grew like
a house emptied of children.

Now the last trace of vanity
scattered, a blond wheel circling her feet.

The dormitory cell   tepid and solitary as death   a hand rubbing
                    over stubble   an hour ago blond waves
        an hour ago   ravished by the joy of denial   alone now
                    a slim body
shivering in the stark white space of a cell.

6. Failing Canonical Year

Not a wrinkle in Father's surplice
Sister Sacristan directed
but keep the iron cool.

Canonical Year, a year to perfect the domestic arts
a year of no study, no books, a year to contemplate

she wondered at night, washing scorches
from her dreams, if anyone could see
through layers and layers of habit the
fruit of her meditation. And the scent

on the other side of the screen as she listed
her sins to Father Confessor, was it
his starched linen collar?
Or was *that* the smell of sex?

Small gestures finished her
days in the kitchen, measuring spoons
spinning from her hands.
Make it level, exact!   All the spilled flour,
all those burnings. *Don't worry* Sister Aimard consoled
we won't leave you alone with the oven.
In the laundry her mind whirled
like washers thrashing white veils
trying to find in each iridescence
those lines she had no time for in her
upstairs notebook. Men write the
old story, a classic rift: Eliot's *Prufrock,*
Augustine's *Confessions.*
Women know another fracturing
all the way down the body.

They found no cause for the fever, but
she had memorized Thomas a Kempis.
A gift from Christ Suffering, she thought,
still the flood of familiar carpings:
anyone can study or write poems.
Hard work is for real women.   A new line
lumined her sleep: *burying brains*
in the garden to see what they sprout.

In the end no one denied it
least of all Sister Mailee.
She had failed canonical year.

7. Retreat

In the notebook next to a muddle about actual grace:
a measure of the degree of disorder . . . entropy
always increases and available energy diminishes

in a closed system.   A shade spills over the facts
when we try to say them, a scrim between story and teller
they shift form like blurred negatives
the thirteen pieces of clothing
I'd worn all those years
                    chemise, pelerine, veil. . .
tossed off that final cell night, a shade over
the facts.   Eighteen years like dominos collapsing.
Terrifying, the quick face of change.

Prepared to descend, I feel for the ground-floor
button of the elevator I had ridden up and down
the years, humming names of the women
I am leaving behind, women who have translated me
who have watched my ivory tower swaying.

Each woman owes her name to another.
I owe mine to many: **Quinnie** who
dangled late afternoon lines of Shakespeare
and quoted Peguy: *my last nickel not for bread but*
white hyacinths.   The novice mistress called her *dangerous.*
We called her *Quinnie.*   Quinnie who knew
I harbored poems.   And made me write them

Sister Marcina of fresh basil and asters
who reminded me, under all that black, I could still feel.
Marcina who sang of *swans by the Oldenburg castle,*
of *young German boyfriends before the Great War*

Sister Inez who introduced Aquinas and
Kierkegaard walking the Flats in Cleveland

Sister Borgias in Asian History class
fleeing her twisted body for the Far East
every Tuesday that last semester and

Pearl Roderick of the Alhambra
Apartment its cockroaches larger than

the first joint of a thumb, Pearl of the Hough Avenue
Project, her six-year-old girl at the back door
that first day: *my mama deaf but she a reader.*
Pearl who saw my dark habit, my
colorless skin and still called me sister.

Most I owe my name to **Mame Padien Brady.**
Mother who comes back in apricot silk
and rain to keep appointments
after death — when there are deadlines.

Afterword:

Be it done to me. A favorite phrase with lots of wives and mothers,
daughters meant to be sons. What a woman won't do for any an-
nouncing angel! Promised divine issue, she'll give all.

In the end the same nightmares: 101 branding my bare back   iced
bodies cubed on conveyor belts   a woman having the same baby
over and over, burying it in the same garden
once I played a circus part, climbed ropes and ran through hoops
of fire   last time I was a hyena   no one could train me to laugh. . . .

Fadings and fates and flowers and female, all the *F* words.
Little ferris wheel friend, what did you know of
fate when you fled that Magnolia home?
what did you know of illusion?

So easy to read these words and
say you had been betrayed, that
what I have written is not you.
The fact is — all these years — I have forgotten
your face. Time fuses. New dolls nest.
More words some day   for now
more blank pages and
these negatives
                    blurred

Three

WE TRIED ON THE UTMOST

for Regina

That day we spoke of Emily
watched her playing with
our minds, hoped to checkmate
always lost in the final stanza.

Not just death, you said, but
death from a terminal illness.
It has to do with terminal illness.
And precisely at that moment
you shed denims for the sheerest
gossamer gown of white and
with a wick your fingers drew
from a left-hand world
you lit the tip of each letter in
the line I had struggled with
for years and the whole poem blazed as
the web around your body vanished.

You sat. You wept miles of muted lines and
we knew somewhere another poem was being
written in flesh disappearing from the face
of a father, a lover
as we tried on the utmost together.

QUINNIE

for Frances Quinlivan

Still her voice dangled late afternoon lines of
Shakespeare, even the tired oak lightened at
her words fine as the gold filigree against autumn
tweeds, cashmere easy on her shoulders.
                    At nineteen we disputed all
truth. Squint, she said and held out
counterfeits. On our mid-west green
with Marx and Aquinas, we walked
that Gothic campus chilled
reading tragedies until our faces grew
into Greek masks, dead heroines traced
on frosted windows. And the French writer:
a last nickel for hyacinths not bread.
Together we tracked origins: seeds, pages
soon whole folios of shimmering flesh
characters waiting to be named under bark
(think of Antigone once in a tree or Caliban or
that Russian woman on the tracks).
We left her passionate to rescue words.

Now older than she was then
(Paganini on broken nights, young odors clinging)
my home shifts through boulders, switchbacks
avalanche country, the Great Divide. In a chaos
far from that early campus Quinnie's green word:
know the genuine.

BIG TESS

on viewing Bernini's painting above the television
—October 15, 1991

Bright on canvas, that Bernini, leaving us
to figure the origin of your wound, you
who loved smooth Cabernet, cream custard, keen
wit: my kind of woman who took on bishops
counseled mystics, audienced with the Pope.
No wonder they named you *Big Tess*
to mark you from the other Saint Therese
the French Carmelite doomed by rose petals
in the eyes of the Fathers who canonized her.
Two women divided by temperament, century, culture.
One when reduced to
the least common denominator.

Today your feast on the catholic saints' calendar
another woman stands at the near end of our century
her not-too-bright cerulean dress fitting
for the glacier mass forming at the front of
the Senate chamber.   An old story:
Susanna, Cassandra, Anita — any name lies
easy on the Fathers' ears bent by tradition.

Come back to us Saint Teresa — Big Tess —
come down from your levitations.
We're burning.

PICTURED LIGHT

radium is not dependent upon an outside source
of energy but appears to arise spontaneously from itself
—adapted from Marie Curie

Picture her worn fingers that night
cold on the doorknob   imagine
the pads of those thumbs near
senseless from chemicals (she was
that in love with looking)
watch her nudge the tentative door of
that converted storeroom lab where
Pierre had helped her search for
imagined light   his own spilling
after the accident to an indifferent Paris
street   consider her nulled
by the French Academy for believing
what she was about to discover, cut
now from her circle of peers like a rare
solitaire sad in an alien gold band
         see her enter the night
     room (in the end — she knew
this — it is all a matter of pictures
making pictures of themselves
in the dark)   see her pupil open
gradual to the unsteady glimmer
that would soon alter worlds much
as any dim heart refusing
         to not glow.

BEFORE HER TIME

Mistress of two lands rich in grace
favorite in the harem of Pharoah,
stone-cutters put down their tools,
her image carved on walls beyond their eyes.

She commanded by her thighs.
After one glance what man could be free
of them? On her ankle white gold
bracelets caught the sun, her keen mind
dazed even the dark philosopher
who felt her spell compelling
the more innocent.

Pharoah knew that point, though,
when all is spoiled. He'd seen the
lotus in the upper valley wither,
in the lower, papyrus keening in the wind.

As legend has it
his wisdom had her
killed before her time.

THE SPELL OF WHIRLPOOL CANYON

It happens to more than queens
that practiced smile until the wife divides
a hair above the heart he commanded
all those years. His guilt, his mourning
commissioned her limestone bust
to be sold to another nation, but
Nefertiti condemned to foreign soil
fled her glass museum and wandered to
a granite niche above new waters.

Now rings of Saturn circle her head like
wedding bands in Whirlpool Canyon. Her
eyes rely on desert varnish for
jet black tears that stream towards
rapids searching for those restless limbs
centuried ago she lost in Egypt's Nile.

CERTAIN WORDS

for Sister Dorothy Kazel murdered in El Salvador, December 2, 1980

The deaths were a matter of chance.
   —Alexander Haig

A fated choice brings us to certain words.
   —Octavio Paz

1

We scan for fragments of you between
shining pages four years folded
in dark leather: *Senior President
Notre Dame Academy Class of '57*
your thin pearls on prom night, blond
hair splayed on a fiancé's shoulder
 our Dorothy *most likely to succeed*

   and traces
on early holy cards tinted girls
   delicate shades from far times
 Cecilia, Agnes, Perpetua
hands crossed over new breasts under tunics
clinging just enough for Roman soldiers.
    At twelve we would emulate them
Be it done to me on their composed faces.

Saints photographed easy then.

2

Eighteen-year-old, from your blue Rambler
Cleveland streets rained a litany of
weathered faces downtown men in
 oversized coats fixed on stone benches play with their
hopeless middle-age on Public Square where
bag ladies feed and feed the pigeons while
  Shaker Heights wives in permanent smiles
  point their Mercedes toward bourbon

tucked between cedar chests furs far from
Hough Avenue where garbage doubles for grass
in Flat #2 Ceil Roderick signs and lipreads,
her smooth ebony hands speaking to six
      hungry children, a husband part-time
           and numbing.

3

Tenacious as slow rain   words change
      a life   no choice you said
      then bartered the diamond on your left hand
for plain silver on the right   to sleep 20 years
alone under convent muslin   your body absent
as white wings over water fonts   absent
as grooves on mahogany prayer stalls where
you cradled predictable *Lives of the Saints*
instead of children in your lap.

4

Those first Salvador snapshots: Juan Pedro
swollen at the collapsed breasts of
15-year-old Rosa   people propped everywhere
against fences   fronts of infirmaries   on the steps of
Escuela Libre. Free. Images. No word
      about killings.

5

A night game   tag   December 2
1980   from the *Aeropuerto*
headlight/lasers searing   polar and deep as
      the last star   a game they called it:
Red-rover   *Red-rover*   *let Sister come over*
      flashlights   5 drunken fireflies
     coding the air
         (and we are
children again   trapping summer
      insects in glass jars   tracking
their bright Ohio release into skies)

        five new games   each had a turn
     in your sex one bullet-wheeze and
          your blond skull exploded . . .
ashes. . . ashes. . . they all fall down).

6
Chalatenango villagers remember bullets
officials denied   *the women broke barricades*
the report read, *the rifles were only to warn them*
     it was a matter of law!
          hour upon hour   *hide-and-seek*
               found: you under leaves
     you   the three others   some blouses backward
     half-a-face blown away   ankles ringed by
underwear, twisted new reports: *just misguided*
soldiers   they will be apprehended
Ambassador White dismissed for: *truth not cover-up*
Alexander Haig: *case closed*

back in safe States   your face
          swelling the screen
     no eye able to hold you
   no shutter to gather the pieces
years later in sleep I rehearse
wild birds violating roses
and your final voice unraveling
on tape: *I am here*
          to give hope
          to the children.

7
Mama!   Mama!   tell my best story again
     about the man who went under the world and
     a locked box just certain words would open.

               No, child. No.
               Tonight's a new story:
          Once upon a time there was this woman . . .

Four

NESTING DOLL

> *. . . memory, you old palimpsest.*
> *—Amy Tan.*

Prelude: How could she know they'd want to stay, all those tenants inside
her   all the dead   all the stillborn and miscarried faces   a din of
voices just before sleep roiling like water or time   in a blue velvet box a
wrong-size birthday amethyst or the complaint of somebody's April coffin
in rain (who hasn't known one?) love on a late Spring side street (trick or
treat   trick or . . .)   still   eyes popping dissonant through trees
pianos exploding black-and-whites that dot the path after the last mourner
> *and what of the watchers*
behind plate-glass on java joint patios   wedged between blinds:
puppets   mimes   anytime people from history   under the bed
rubber playmates hiding   any mouth capable of saying or singing
will all she remembers tumble the grave after her?

Storyteller:
Pop her open and watch
the figures pour out of themselves
girl-doll by girl-doll each a brooding
replica except a feature here, a gesture:
one is inviting, another covers her ears
a third frowns as though thinking too much
and the arms of a fourth meld, waiting
whatever will happen in her torso, finally
the last-carved always visible one
that ultimate mummer protecting each from
herstory.
                    They dare us by their eyes
to release those faces buried in tapestries
above our mantles, cramped in bronze frames
hiding or buried deep in the family plot.
        All remembered in the
quaint nesting doll on that shelf, mumming.

I am distinct from *we are.*

First Doll:
August 15, 1930
I write while the baby sleeps, Claire. On her back. In the crib. I am careful
with this one after all those lost tadpoles and the one that came out dead and
the one we put in the ground the third day. Still I feel her already leaving.
Such mystery. The egg is made flesh. A simple process really. It's all
about eggs. One of them stays, clings. Where do the rest go? Eggs in, eggs
out. A woman separates and is no longer one. She is outside herself.
Watching. Is that why men envy us, Claire? Is that why they try to make
us their bodies?

Second Doll:
Under a faint light at Ocean Grove
a blond girl-child digging gold sand

barely enough hand for fragments of
shell   and at the water-edge

waiting her   the white gull
        (a rush of holy feathers
often a sweep of wings at the ear
whispers almost clear enough to catch
the only audible sound
        grief flapping its mad measure)

First Doll:
December 12, 1932

        The Bradys are devouring me, Claire. I'm being shaped to a sounding board by Katie and Annie. And Ma Brady's obsession is Alec: "God graced me. He gave me a boy." It's understandable. Five children, no money and still in her twenties when Thomas died, and the terror of his body in half on the tracks. The girls fight like Irish urchins for what's left of Ma's affection. I end up always in the middle. Ma won't wear anything but the sturdy "old country" flannels, won't hear it when the girls talk about lighter undies. Something about modesty.

        The laundry's heavy and my hands collapse easily, Claire. Katie bought one of those hand wringers, said I could come by her house the days I washed Ma's things. But I'd have to cart the wet clothes back down Franklin Turnpike to Lincoln Place to dry them on our line.

        Six days a week at the office and Alec's exhausted. Sundays after Mass he just wants to numb in his armchair. That's why we don't visit all of you more. It's a long drive from Waldwick to Patterson. The youngest Brady sister Nellie brings her family up from the City and the wives take turns with Sunday dinner. The tension when we're together is so thick I keep a close watch on who's carving the lamb or beef or pork poast. I wish Alec and I could get away alone some week ends.

        Lately I'm always tired, Claire. And sad. Very sad. The doctors call it "melancholia nervosa." During the day Ma and the children need caring. There's no alone place. None. Sometimes I think my dark thoughts might have killed the four who should have been babies. After the stillborn I tried to change. I keep wondering if I got enough rest those nine months, if I ate the right things, or whether I was too homesick and grieving. (They say things like that can kill what's trying to grow inside). Something made Alec Jr.'s little heart fail after just three days. Alec says I shouldn't blame myself but then he goes on about our latest not being the son he wanted. He'll never get over the loss. I'll never get over feeling the fault.

Storyteller:
Centuries ago that monk brought home
the first Russian doll nesting
all the way back from China. How long
had he carried her inside? how long
had she waited the hollowed birch
or lime to release her?

Third Doll:
Sick with scarlet fever when they buried my bird without me. At five
my first death parlor. At seven, my bird. Last year two friends I
keep digging up. This morning I wrote: So that's what death is —
someone no longer holding me here — some eye no longer looking.
Someone looks long at my body and I am whole again. No divine
plan, just one eye and another.

Second Doll:
one brick missing from the wall on Belmore Road
size fours trying to scale it, boosting
her little girl body that comes down a 50-year-old.
At 18 she returns in search of that brick.
        At 36. At 49.
Sometimes at night she still climbs
under the blue-and-red wallpaperchildren
the girl suspended mid-air.
the boys turning rope, watching her
skip double-Dutch into sleep.

Fourth Doll:
But that isn't mother at the cutting
board, spreading sandwiches for
my lunch box each morning
the hands are far too small, hands
that polished and polished silver for
parties we never had.

First Doll:

July 6, 1964

I never wanted his sterling silver, never wanted the quiet apricot cushions by the Cleveland bay window, the oak-paneled dining room he worked so hard for. I never wanted his Magnolia house. I stirred years of cream in Instant Nescafe, numbed by pretend-always neighbors, longing to break my crystal and bone china bonds and the Russian olives outside our breakfast nook window greened and grayed with the seasons. I dreamed onion skin paper to wrap around myself, ink to drown myself in and the word's perverse consolation, not the tranquilizing phrases he vowed would make me well. In the end I settled for the sad amber glass.

Fourth Doll:

Why do we grieve our dolls so long even after they've rotted?

He had a way of severing
words at their roots, the man
she chose to honor and obey.
Even after he silenced my
favorite doll in the permanent dumpster
her bright rubber mouth told all
the red secrets hidden from me:
      the little girl downstairs who swelled and went away
      the little boy who didn't see the car coming
and on the circular stair mother
of the Magnolia house, swaying.

First Doll:

July 15, 1948

Why does she want to leave this soon, Claire? my beautiful sea-girl? Did I confide too much those breakfast nook mornings? Most nights Alec was always too tired to listen. He'd talk about Jim Tobin's temper flares or Mike Fahey's drinking and "that thieving Louie Di Paula." All night. Next morning I couldn't stop talking to our youngest. From the time she was five. Once when I was making flaxseed poultices for her boils I told her: never marry. When we'd travel down home to Paterson from Cleveland

she'd see me with the rest of you and ask: Mama how come you don't laugh
like this at home? how come you don't do your hair at home in crawlers?
She'd play with words and make me smile. There's so much of our family in
her, Claire, but Alec's too . . . never finished with sacrifice and suffering.
Always loving too much. I don't think she'll survive the convent. She'll
change her mind.

September 15, 1948

Dear Claire,
She left last week. Said she had a call from God, a vocation. You'd think
she's hearing voices? I don't want another Joan on my hands. One of us is
enough in a family.

I can't write anymore just now. My vision's blurring.

February 22, 1949

Dear Claire,
The beautiful bed jacket came today. It's perfect for bitter Cleveland days.
And you know I love aquamarine. We get only three-hour visits every six
weeks. And no phone calls. Last time I'd saved some things to tell, waited
until all her friends left. In the middle of one of my stories the convent bell
rang. She made me stop, stood up at the first chime, said the bell was God's
voice. That sent me spiraling for weeks. I'm some better now. The doctor
calls it grieving. I tried to tell him nobody died.

Second Doll:

(if you're gonna' do it do it at least in the roses)   All the same
script   same faces from central casting   the beach party
Sister Gerard condemned in tenth grade   the white swim suit
that almost took her under   foreign tongues intruding
more often these days she's wrapped in black serges
  beginning to ask which voice is right   beginning to mistrust
        the one that spells J - O - Y
   to tremble as the one whispers: covet the thorns, sex is an enemy
      don't you forget it   later, much later: the forbidden
cloister tears   better to blame Christ's passion
                than her own   her own
                    now burning.

Storyteller:
When he asked her name
she said *I am water.*

Fifth Doll:
Pleasure under the spigot
in the old porcelain tub, its
feet clawing the black and white
octagon tiles of my initiation room: first
nosebleeds, first destination for
those flushed unknown fish and
the first stains not prepared for

are we ever prepared — the original
coupling: fear and desire?
do we ever stop asking *where does it lead?*
          last night at dinner the woman's
sheer voile, she has become
me, showing just enough breast,
tossing her hair, bending — a laser — to
each conversation across white linen and crystal
                    (think of the artifice   think of the pose)

First Doll:
Yes.   That woman has become me
who writes letters in seductive fonts
wears apricots and violets from Victoria
then turns cold, forgets the altogether-hunt
loses the language

Second Doll:
and that sea girl becomes me
bends with hot longing
each year to the Ocean Grove tide
trying to hide in a Fourth of July mist
no firecracker would dare
          sometimes wishing herself
an orphan stone, a misplaced rock

beside honeysuckle undressing in air
suffused with words foreign to her tongue

Fourth Doll:
and that one draped in black, denying
herself, the woman of smoked reflections
whose lips form *maybe* for *never,*
I'm sorry for *damn you,* who won't leave
her father's bones alone in
the Ridgewood, New Jersey grave,
that woman too has become me
      who wears this face
        who is insatiable
          behind those famished lips
     a wilder appetite for a fresh ethic
          an original aesthetics
          a brand new poetics

Second Doll:
Never the real face, right?
How can the same body that weeps
over Bosnian children
worry the right shade lipstick
the best vanishing cream? the same
ear that courts angels and Holocaust
ghosts, drown in departmental gossip? how
can the tongue keep repeating last year
when last year lies down in her now
playing hide-and-seek with the dead?

Words flit down a hall stinging
(so self-satisfied they say)
past nameplates with no one behind them,
in a cramped room two figures hunch over
semi-colons, worrying categories and
the importance of the chairman, singing
thanks for their fraudulent supper, mouthing
stale parodies, leaving

Bartok and John Cage irrelevant, and
　　　　Hildegard von Bingen.

(The matryushka is smiling the madmothersmile.)

. . . *self-satisfied* they say.
I say ask the doll inside.

Sixth Doll:
dear mama/god,
i wan outta here
i donlike the neighbors
i wanna be
where i can see
where i can say
whadiwanna:
blankiepuppie
　　　　waaahhh!
i wanna be out there not crowded in your middle,
　　　　　　i wanna flap my arms
　　　　　　　　　　play bird
　　　　　　not
stand-straight-hands-at-sides
　　　i wanna sing　　wanna grow faces
　you can't count on
fingers and toes　　　'n play letters 'til they hum
umm　　yeh　hummmm

dear mama/god
　　　i
wanna turn 'n turn 'til
like big sister says
 all my juices
　　jazz

Seventh Doll:
Don't expect an ending that will keep the flies away.　It's all a matter of
entropy, ya' know.　All about momentum and loss.　Every time.　Still we

all like a little schmaltz, right? Always have. A little pretend. We try so
long to run from who we are. History should be more convincing.
Outrageous isn't it! A first breath, all the rest so shallow as if not to disturb
by taking in air. Lives spent struggling to fit.

No, you say ? No? You in Loge B. You say you're content with
who you are? Usher, show him out. He doesn't belong. The rest of us
know. One denial after another.

Second Doll:
(I am water
she said when he asked her name)

Say what you mean. Your words are opaque.
I know what I mean by saying: Havasupai
from Rt. 66 in our *Explorer* I am
already undressing under the Falls.

Eight miles down   then sleep
at the reservation   next day the hike to Mooney Falls
high at its source a split bush, at bottom sandstone
cliffs jut like petrified lace making me come
back to the haunted forests of childhood
teeming with moss, green and promising
as female desire

a steep descent
few footholds, only cold lethargic
chains to guide our hands down the
sheer wall masquerading as a path
        I am already sick from fear of
the long climb out. Still we are here
the Falls singing their fractured
music, miming all
the bright flying creatures, on
the sand bar, two blue dragonflies
twinning in air.
        How can anyone say goodbye
to this beauty? Once I resisted
rafting the Green River but

one of the dolls said *do* and I did
then ran the Grand Canyon's Colorado
          another   and another all the way
to Peru's Urubamba, Kenya's Mara.
In the end though
truth lies in the day-by-day
between exotic journeys
in the dash between dates on the headstone

still there's a world out there and
I don't want to turn into a book.

A faint shimmer from the slit around
the middle of my Russian matryushka
her eyes no longer fixed to one side
from each black lash
a Gershwin flutter, as though
had she feet she would spring wild into
the Charleston her mother never got to do.

Storyteller:
Putting them back one by one

Sixth Doll:
the smallest — first-carved — shaping the rest:

Third Doll:
the size, the look around the mouth

First Doll:
how tall, how steep each will descend

Fourth Doll:
and whether the ascent will be
toe by toe and assiduous

Second Doll:
or whether barefoot
she will fly

Fifth Doll:
how our lips don't want to part
for   *love   good-bye   longing*
how other words split the palate
                              negotiate
                              deal
                              punish
                    (she shall be punished they cried
when her sex popped out).

To fear loving too much, not enough
         being loved and not being.
I know you will understand she says
finding each time no one can.

Storyteller:
Like the fairy tale we follow the crumbs home to
a chaos bright on the nursery floor, remember?
Even now each time we begin in that cave
behind the eye we hear
the first alphabet humming.

Notes

Pictured Light. The words of the epigraph found in Eve Curie's biography of her mother first appeared in Marie Curie's notebooks.

Last Song. I owe the inspiration for this poem to Kathleen Raine's work on mandalas.

Like This. At a writers' retreat in Telluride, Colorado, I was introduced to the work of the Persian poet Rumi.

Female Jesuits from *Certain Words*. Simone Weil's remark is found in *Waiting for God*.   The stanza from Sor Juana's poem 37 appears in the *Sor Juana Anthology* edited by Alan Trueblood.

Monologue. The epilogue is taken from William Kennedy's *Ironweed*.

Certain Words. The substance of Alexander Haig's comment appeared in several news releases at the time of the killings in El Salvador. Octavio Paz's statement is found in more than one of his writings, most notably in *Convergences*.

Nesting Doll: *Prelude*. The epigraph is taken from Amy Tan's *The Hundred Secret Senses*.

DATE DUE

UPI 261-2505 G   PRINTED IN U.S.A.